Dear God ...

Letters from the Nursing Home

by

Mary-Ellen Low

Dear God ... Letters from the Nursing Home

All Rights Reserved © 2013 by Mary-Ellen Low

No part of this book may be reproduced or transmitted in any form or by any means, graphic, electronic, or mechanical, including photocopying, recording, taping, or by any information storage retrieval system without the written permission of the author.

For information call: 304-285-8205
or Email: acornbookservices@comcast.net

This book is a work of fiction. Names, characters, places, and incidents are products of the author's imagination or are used fictitiously. Any resemblance to actual events or locales or persons, living or dead, is entirely coincidental.

Designed by Acorn Book Services

Publication Managed by Acorn Book Services
www.acornbookservices.com
acornbookservices@gmail.com
304-285-8205

Illustrated by Nicole Rose

Cover designed by Todd Aune
Spokane, Washington
www.projetoonline.com

ISBN-10: 0985726792
ISBN-13: 978-0-9857267-9-9

Printed in the United States of America

This book is dedicated to Marylou with love:

*She's someone who knows every dream you pursue,
What you think, how you feel, why you do what you do.
She's someone who knows the most innermost you
And loves who you are....she's your sister.*

Acknowledgements

I have been blessed in my life to have worked with some of the finest nurses and nursing assistants long-term care has to offer. The time and love they devote to their careers and their nursing home residents are immeasurable. These men and women stand for the right to live peacefully and with joy as well as the right to die with dignity. My life has been enriched because of our time together. There is a special place in heaven for these heroes of long-term care nursing.

My heartfelt thanks to author, Lauren Carr, my editor and publisher. She had faith in my ability to write a book and put in an incredible amount of time and passion to create a book worth publishing. Plus, she enjoys a hot cup of coffee or hot chocolate at our favorite eatery, Panera Bread. I swear, ideas just start to flow while drinking one of their delightful beverages!

I would like to thank Sarah Gratz for the outstanding picture she took of the beautiful ladies who grace the back cover of this book. Stay with nursing, Sarah. Your heart is in the right place for it.

I would like to extend a very special thanks to "Jeff" Jeffers. He was my friendly reader and had great insights and provided help I truly appreciated and needed. The last letter titled "A Letter from Jeff" is his own beautiful, personal love story to God about him and his wife, Anne. He was an inspiration, not just to me, but to each nurse he came in contact with at the nursing home. A man with his qualities comes along once in a lifetime.

Todd Aune designed the cover of my book. Thank you, Todd, for your creative talents. I'd take you to Panera Bread, too, but you live so far away. Much success with your future endeavors. Maybe I'll need your talent again in another 10 years or so. I'm a slow writer.

To Nicole Rose, my illustrator, I can only say, "You amaze me." You manage a balancing act of full-time nursing work, a husband, a house full of beautiful and energetic kids, attending sporting events and other duties like it's a piece of cake. Where you squeezed in the time to do such a top-notch job with the book's illustrations, I'll never know. Your positive spirit is something I greatly admire. You are the best and I love you.

In closing, I'd like to offer my deepest gratitude to my sister, Marylou, and my husband, Bob. You listened to my letters with kind encouragement and gentle criticism. Marylou, you are my best friend and a strong supporter. Plus, there's no one in the world that makes me crack up laughing like you do. How many times when we're together do I have to plead with you to stop making me laugh so I don't wet my pants? Remember the store with the hot sauces with the funny names that we got thrown out of for carrying on too much? I wish we lived next door to one another instead of five hours apart.

Bob, you are the love of my life from day one. Together 34 years and counting. Where did the time go? Let's retire soon and spend the rest of our lives with our babies, Tilly and Bella, at the beach. Cottage Café here we come!

Table of Contents

A Letter from Mary-Ellen 13
A Letter from John 16
A Letter from Cecelia 19
A Letter from Belle 21
Letter from Nikki 26
A Letter from Eleanor 29
A Letter from Terence 32
A Letter from Vickie 37
A Letter from Sabrina 41
A Letter from Tilly 43
A Letter from Eva 45
A Letter from Sissy 49
A Letter from Helen 54
A Letter from Lottie 56
A Letter from Jenny 61
A Letter from Gerda 66
A Letter from Jack 70
A Letter from Gordon 72
A Letter from Freddie 75
A Letter from Oscar 80
A Letter from Betty 83
A Letter from Becky 86
A Letter from Sally 90
A Letter from Bonnie's Friends 92
A Letter About Lucy 95
A Letter from Bobby 99

A Letter from Gertie 104
A Letter from Ellie 106
A Letter from Laura 108
A Letter from Mary 113
A Letter from Sidney 115
A Letter from Mickey 117
A Letter from Sharon 121
 A Letter from Virginia 125
A Letter from Julie 127
A Letter from Arianne 131
A Letter from Jeff 136
Pearls of Wisdom
from the Nursing Home 145
Top Ten Things
My Nursing Training Never Prepared Me For
In My Long-Term Nursing Career 147
Gift Ideas for
Nursing Home Residents 150
Favorite Recipes
from the Nursing Home Staff 154
About the Author 168
About the Illustrator 168

Aged spirits whose mortal shells bear the scars of a tumultuous life send their voices unto the heavens while housed within these caring walls. Their deliberate song rises to the ears of a loving God weaving the story of their lives wherein the underlying message of a desire to ascend to His throne room resides.

Shaun Mitchem

Dear God ...

Letters from the Nursing Home

Letters from the Nursing Home

A Letter from Mary-Ellen

Dear God,

My former patient, John, has returned for admission to the nursing home today. I'm his admitting nurse. I'm so very happy to see him again but, sadly, I know this means he has to give up living on his own permanently this time.

John has always reminded me of a warrior. Even though he has advanced Parkinson's disease, he battles his diagnosis with every fiber of his being. I remember how his limbs used to become "frozen" when his medication stopped working, and he would fall to his knees. But instead of calling for help, he preferred to pop a pill and wait until he became "unfrozen" then get up on his own power.

Dear God ...

During his last admission, John and I fought very hard to get him discharged home, even if his stay there only lasted two to three months. A staff meeting took place with the care plan team, John, and his daughter, Carolyn, present. John spoke with passion about how he had to prove to himself that he still had some fight left. That the disease hadn't won. He and I were both of the mind that without this final chance at independence, he would never be able to accept a permanent nursing home placement.

Somehow with his impassioned pleas and his daughter's backup, a decision was made to send him home. On the day John left, I gave him a small plastic figure of a superhero. "This reminds me of you, John----courageous and strong-willed with a fight for independence against great odds. I'm so proud of you." He laughed and put the action figure in his suitcase.

Well, two years have passed and John arrived back today. He seems smaller and less capable physically, but his spirit continues to flourish. In his customary military style, he saluted me and

Letters from the Nursing Home

greeted me by name. "Mary-Ellen, I've given it my best shot and now I'm reporting for my final assignment," he said.

On his dresser, among family pictures and other treasures, was his superhero. Seeing this brought tears to my eyes, God.

When John dies, I will ask his daughter if I may keep the plastic superhero. For me it will be an ultimate reminder of what courage and heroism is all about. Welcome home, John.

With Admiration and Pride,

Mary-Ellen

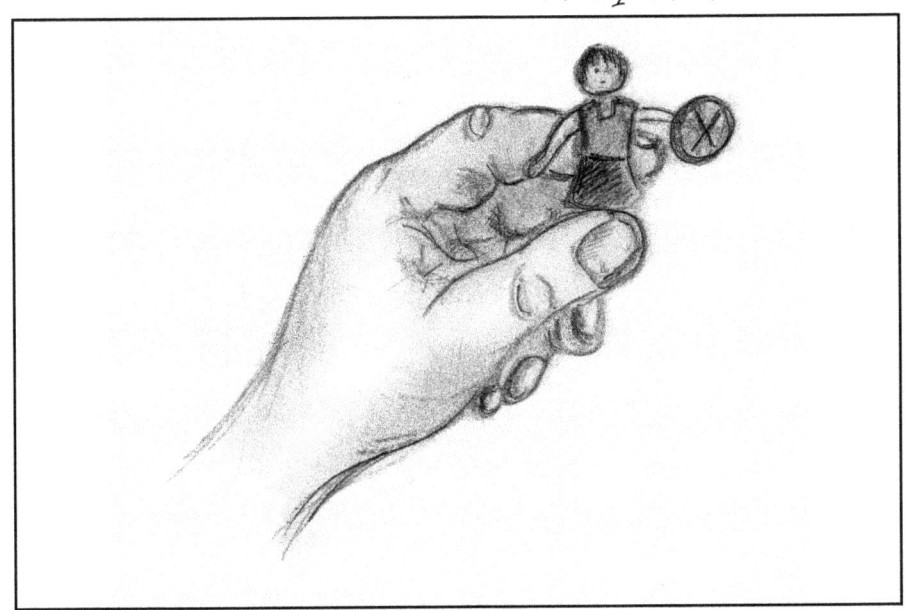

Dear God ...

A Letter from John

Dear God,

It's not easy to grow old and it's even harder to do so with Parkinson's disease. I've battled this enemy—the most determined enemy of my life as a soldier—and I've fought harder than I've ever fought against anyone or anything. It's finally brought me to a long-term nursing home and then here to the Health Services Center—my "final assignment".

But, as hard as it is to be here, to acknowledge that I'm losing the fight against my terrible enemy, I have to thank You, God, that my final years are here in this place. I am surrounded by other people who have spent their lives, like I have, serving their country. That has been a real comfort and I have made some good friends in this place.

Letters from the Nursing Home

Even more important to me have been the wonderful staff here. Where did You find these people, God? They are angels and their kindness and gentle care make Your love ever present to me. My favorite, though, is Mary-Ellen. She fought for me so that I could have more time living in my own apartment in the more independent part of this nursing facility. For that, I'll always be grateful to her. She, more than anyone else, recognized the fighter in me and did everything she could to help me fight on.

Now that I'm in the midst of my final battle, she is still by my side. She is a wonderful nurse----- she makes sure that everything is done for me and done well. She is always doing whatever it takes to make me comfortable.

Dear God ...

I'm grateful to her for so much, but especially for her kindness, her complete honesty, and for her unrelenting good humor. And I'm grateful that she has also been such a good friend to my daughter, Carolyn, and to my old friends, Ben and Rosemary.

Dear God, please bless Mary-Ellen. She has made such a difference in my life. May her future be filled with joy and peace. Most of all, may she know how much comfort she brings and how much love she shares. If she could know this, I know she would be a happy nurse. And, she deserves that!

Your Faithful Friend,

John

Letters from the Nursing Home

A Letter from Cecelia

Dear God,

    I live in the Shady Pines Nursing Home. Would it be wrong for me to get a mouse trap to set inside my closet to catch a thief? I don't want to hurt anyone, truly I don't. But in the past month I've "lost" two pairs of fuzzy slippers, a Jaclyn Smith sweater, my denture adhesive, a racy novel, three jars of anti-wrinkle cream, and my only bra (48 DDD).

Dear God ...

I believe I know who the thief is. She's a cleaning lady who is built like Dolly Parton. Her skin has looked remarkably smooth this week thanks to my miracle cream. I've seen her leaving the nursing home with a pocketbook the size of a piano. I am sure that I'm not the only one missing precious belongings.

    Praying for an Answer to My Dilemma,

    Cecelia

P.S. She can keep the racy novel. I have read it three times already. God forgive me.

    Thanks Again,

    C.

Letters from the Nursing Home

A Letter from Belle

Dear God,

I've recently come to realize that I am an education fanatic. I have spent a lifetime pursuing my studies and have always loved to learn. My husband often accuses me of being obsessed with academia. He's dubbed me, "the eternal student." I have just completed my third doctorate, this one in philosophy. I also love linguistics and speak four languages fluently. I'm not bragging, God, this is just who I am.

My most recent educational pursuit has been cut short by a massive coronary at the age of 53. I spent 2 weeks in the nearby teaching hospital connected to every tube and wire imaginable. Now here I sit in a nursing home for what they call "reconditioning." It's as though I'm a run-down

Dear God ...

vehicle in need of a major tune-up. I guess that's true.

Anyway, I was determined to keep to myself while here. Surely mingling with the aged population that represents the majority of the clients would have no benefit for someone like me. But, being the pompous ass that I am, this did nothing but help me sink into a self-centered depression.

An astute nurse realized all my classic symptoms and advised me to do some sorely needed socializing. "Have supper in the main dining hall" she recommended.

So against my better judgement and with all the mental strength I could muster, I complied. Surprisingly, this challenged my thinking about myself, my education, and the multiple purposes of a nursing home stay.

I was warmly invited to table #1 where the welcoming committee sat. Six women and a single man were awaiting supper. They greeted me like I was royalty. Before the meal started, Esta said,

Letters from the Nursing Home

"It's time to pray". We all joined hands and she said, "Thank You, Lord, for our newest guest. May she enjoy our company, tolerate the food, and have a speedy recovery from the illness that brings her to our home."

Then, each person went around the table and told God what they were thankful for that day. The answers were interesting and heart-warming. Ann broke the reverent mood by thanking God for "the bitchy nurse being off duty for a week".

When it came to my turn, I was surprised to find I was at no loss for words or sentiments. "I'm thankful for seven new friends. And knowing that bad food eaten with friends is so much better than great food eaten alone. I am grateful to the nurse who knew my best medicine would not come from a pill, but rather in companionship and sharing."

While everyone applauded my answers, I continued to think: "Some of my best learning has come from stepping outside my ego and taking part in life wherever I find myself."

Dear God ...

So, God, You are probably thinking: "OK, you spent one meal with others. Did you go back into your shell for the rest of your stay?"

The answer is an absolute and resounding "NO." After my daily routine and therapies, I went to work on my self-improvement. I read letters to visually impaired residents. I played bingo for the first time in my life (and won a giant box of Mike and Ike candy). I attended wheelchair exercise sessions, quiz day, and arts and crafts where I made a tiara, which I wore to the nursing home New Year's Eve celebration. And at the party, I joined in the group toast with apple cider and cookies. I took a silent pledge to myself that weekly nursing home visits would become part of my New Year's resolution. Because, God, as my husband says, I am an eternal student. And learning to play with others, share yourself and embrace life in every part of the journey is all part of my rock solid education.

Still Learning,

Belle

Letters from the Nursing Home

Dear God ...

A Letter from Nikki

Hi, God,

It's your friend, Nikki. I went to see my Nana today. She lives in a place like a hospital, but they say it's her new home. Mom called it a nursing home. So many of the people were very, very old, like Nana.

She was so happy to see me that she cried. What surprised me was that so many of the people who lived there were happy to see me, too. Old people I never even saw before smiled at me and many of them tried to hug me. It was like they hadn't seen a little girl for a long time or something.

I spent 45 minutes with a group of women in an art class. I fit right in

Letters from the Nursing Home

because most of them didn't draw or paint any better than I do.

   I painted a picture of my dog, Dakota, and gave it to a very tiny lady in a wheelchair. She got tears in her eyes and clung to the picture like it was something very special. I mean, my art teacher at school probably wouldn't even have given me a "B" on it, but she seemed to really love it.

   I was thinking, God. Do old people in nursing homes miss seeing kids? Maybe I should visit again soon and bring some of my friends. We could sing and play games and have a happy time. It might help them forget their problems. Do old people like pizza and soda like I do? How about chewy candy and cheese doodles (my favorites)?

Dear God ...

I think I'll go back next week with my mom to see Nana. It looks like a lot more people than Nana would be happy to see me, especially the tiny wheelchair lady. I'll ask her for her name next time. That'll make her feel special.

                                    Your Friend,
                                    Nikki
                                  (Sparta, NJ)

Letters from the Nursing Home

A Letter from Eleanor

Dear God,

You have been a part of my life since day one, since conception. You are The Almighty One, all knowing, all seeing, all powerful. The past, the present, and the future are one with You. So, it is with great trepidation that I ask this question: "Why am I not among Your chosen in heaven?"

I have lived a devoted Christian life. And I do appreciate the long and wonderful life I have experienced, but I turned 105 this past January. My mind is still pretty sharp. But, my body is worn to a frazzle, literally. The nurses say my voice sounds like long nails scratching along a blackboard. My skin has the consistency of parchment paper. I'm not exaggerating. I get a skin tear if someone so much as looks at me too long.

Dear God ...

God, don't think I don't appreciate the life I've been given. It has been a long and very privileged journey. I prided myself in owning one of the first cars made in America. I loved to travel and I've driven, flown, trained,  and boated, as well as been chauffeured to too many places to recall. I graduated from a very elite college, well before women graduating with a four-year degree was common place. I have known and dined with more famous people than a rock star.

Since my life was so busy, I didn't find love until the ripe old age of 50. When I finally did, it was a deep and abiding love. My only sadness stems from never having a child. This is truly my only regret.

I have been in this nursing home for 6 years. The care is quality and the staff is top-notch, but the monotony of it all gets to me. I call it the seven-question daily grind:

1. Do you want eggs or cereal for breakfast?

Letters from the Nursing Home

   2. Do your dentures fit?

   3. Do you want to eat alone or in the main dining hall? (with a group of people I can no longer see or hear)

   4. Do you want to wear a nightgown or hospital gown to bed?

   5. Bed bath or shower bath? (how about no bath today? How dirty can I get doing nothing all day?)

   6. Did you poop today? (How much more embarrassing can this get?)

   7. Would you like a pet visit today?

Lord, I'm beyond ready to experience the wonder of You. So, remember me when You are seeking to bring home one of Your faithful devotees. One hundred and five years is a long time to wait for our reunion.

                                    Yours From Day One,

                                        Eleanor

Dear God ...

A Letter from Terence

Dear God,

For some reason beyond all human understanding, I'm still here. Meaning I'm still alive.

Last Friday, Father William returned home to the rectory after his trip to Tennessee to visit his parents. He found me on the floor of the rectory chapel pale, passed out and lifeless. Without hesitation, 911 was called and I was whisked off to the hospital with sirens blasting. They tell me I flat-lined in the ambulance and had to be resuscitated. Another heart attack. The first at age twenty-four and now, again, at the age of fifty-five.

I'm recovering here at the local nursing home. I have rigorous strength training for my heart

Letters from the Nursing Home

and additional therapy for my fractured ankle. I'm pushed to my cardiac limits and, God, I know it's for my own good, but I'm simply wiped out. There's a self-imposed limit on the number of visitors and time they may stay to prevent any further exhaustion. This way I don't have my entire congregation barraging the place, as well meaning as they might be. After all, I am here to recover.

Dear God ...

God, frankly I'm confused. I feel I shouldn't question Your divine wisdom, but why didn't You let me die? Is there something in my priestly duties that I've yet to accomplish?

I've been praying for days for some insight into my experience and what I must learn from it. There has been so much published regarding near death phenomena. Well, I've had two major cardiac events with near-death experiences, but I draw a total blank when I attempt to recall a tunnel of light or a Godly being giving me direction. I recall nothing. I only know what Father William has told me.

My nurse tells me that my forgetting everything around my cardiac arrest may well be "the wisdom of the body". She said my mind has emptied itself of stressful information so it can begin the work of healing. This does make a lot of sense.

So, as I spend my time here recovering, I'm praying for the strength and peace needed to go forward with my priestly duties.

Letters from the Nursing Home

I've learned a lot from the nursing home staff. As stressful as their workload and long hours are, they seem to have found a home in their career choice. They are attentive to my needs, but they like to have fun and try to lighten up my serious nature. For instance, last night's meal was almost unrecognizable. "

"What is on my tray tonight?" I questioned.

My CNA said, "Oh, that's F.U.O., short for Food of Unknown Origin."

We laughed together and she offered to get me another meal choice, but didn't guarantee that it would be any more recognizable that the first selection.

God, I'm trying to use my time here to develop ideas to expand my ministry to involve the community. It may be spiritually satisfying to me to do nursing home visits for residents having trouble adapting to nursing home placement and staffers that might need support in a stressful career.

Dear God ...

Father William saved my life though he's too modest to take any credit. He has always been my mentor. He taught me it is important to leave my mark while on this earth by bringing the love and joy of knowing God and His son, Jesus, to all who come across my path. God, I plan to be open to new ways as well as new places to share Your everlasting love. Amen.

Your Humble Servant,

Terence

Letters from the Nursing Home

A Letter from Vickie

Dear God,

Is it possible to be addicted to Bingo? I know it's a silly old game, but I think it's become my obsession. I get so depressed on non-Bingo days, I don't even leave my room. I've named my precious twin Chihuahuas "Free Space" and "B6". Last Tuesday night, I screamed "Bingo" in my sleep and nearly awakened the aide asleep in my Lazy Boy lounge chair. Then I remembered the most bizarre dream.

In my dream, an angel appeared before me at a Bingo table. I know he was an angel because he had feathery wings and Brad Pitt's face, so I wouldn't exactly call it a nightmare. Anyway, he said, "You will

Dear God ...

never win at Bingo because you don't follow the Ten Commandments of Nursing Home Bingo". He repeated the following over and over until I had them memorized:

1. Thou shalt not scream, "Oh, God, why me?" every time you lose a game.

2. Thou shalt not skip out on Sunday service or hymn practice for Bingo attendance.

3. Thou shalt not spill fruit punch on your neighbor's Bingo card when they are about to win.

4. Thou shalt not sit in your neighbor's lucky seat when they leave for the john.

5. Thou shalt not steal anyone's Bingo cards, chips, or prizes.

6. Thou shalt not run over the winning player in your wheelchair.

7. Thou shalt not feign a heart attack to end any game you are not winning.

8. Thou shalt not play footsie with your roommate's boyfriend during a game.

9. Thou shalt not wear your "I'm the Bingo Queen" shirt on game days.

10. Thou shalt not call Bingo "the game from hell" every time you lose.

Dear God ...

God, this dream scared the life out of me. Do I need psychiatric help? Should I attend a Bingo Anonymous support group?

                Newly Retired Bingo Queen,
                    Vickie

Letters from the Nursing Home

A Letter from Sabrina

Dear God,

I woke up mad at You today. You see, I'm no longer in good health and my husband is even frailer than I am. He is now wheelchair-bound and a stroke has robbed him of his speaking voice. We're in a nursing home in different wings and different floors. This is the first time in our 60-year marriage that we are apart and it breaks my heart. My will to care for him is strong but my physical strength is gone. And, yet.....

Today, late in the day before sunset, we sat outside together for one hour with the sun warming our faces. No conversation, yet in

Dear God ...

peaceful communion with one another. A feeling of serenity came over me and I realized three things:

I'm still with the love of my life.
The world is truly beautiful to behold.
Our God loves us.

Then I forgot why I was so mad at You.

Still Your Friend,

Sabrina

Letters from the Nursing Home

A Letter from Tilly

Dear God,

I think You have a very warped sense of humor. I mean just look at me! I'm 89 years old and only part of me is still left here on earth. For how long and for what reason I ask You?

Let me spell it out for You. So far, there are only three teeth left in my head. The rest sit in a glass on my bedside stand each night. I have an artificial knee joint and a heart valve replacement. I have no tonsils, no gall bladder, no appendix, no uterus, only one breast and very little hair. Six skin cancers have been removed. Diabetes took 2 toes and a bleeding ulcer caused me to have half of my stomach surgically extracted. My cataracts were removed last year. I have no sense of taste or smell and only 50% of my vision.

Dear God ...

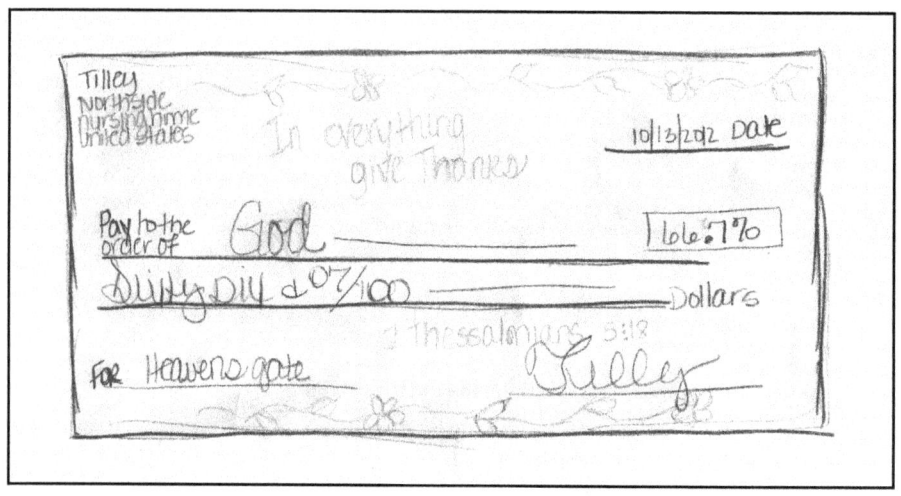

To sum it all up, 33% of my body no longer exists. Gone. Kaput.

If I were a car, I would have been towed to the junk yard. If I were a building, I'd have been dynamited!

As Scottie would say, "Beam me up".

Please, God, I'm ready for You to take the other 66.7% of me home to heaven. And I hope You still recognize me when the time comes.

Hopefully Yours,

Tilly

Letters from the Nursing Home

A Letter from Eva

Dear God,

I've been a spectacle my whole life—a circus attraction, really. The fat lady in the circus, that's me. Tipping the scale at just over 400 lbs. has been the hardship of my life. A fat child, a fat teenager, and now a grossly fat adult.

I fell and broke my pelvis two weeks ago and it took six strong men to get me onto the stretcher and out the front door to the hospital. Luckily, no surgery was needed. I'm now involved in three weeks of bed rest, and then therapy at the local nursing home where I am currently.

I have been glared at with disgust because of my girth most of my adult life. I expected that the nursing home staff would show a little

Dear God ...

sympathy being that they deal with illness and diseases out of the norm. Some of the nursing aides are fresh out of school and have limited training.

I heard two young aides out in the hallway, just outside my door, laughing hysterically. I was the brunt of their joke. They were recollecting how they were almost bowled over by my flubbery

Letters from the Nursing Home

abdomen when they turned me on my side this morning.

Imagine my embarrassment. I cried with shame most of the day.

A lovely woman named Serena was my evening aide. She was both experienced and compassionate. During her hands-on care, she looked me right in the eye and I could feel there was no judgement.

I told her about my earlier experience with the young girls who made fun of me.

She told me how some of the inexperienced CNAs love to make fun of everyone and everything. "You should hear them carry on about the dietary staff and the older nurses. They are relentless. They make fun of each other, too. Their self-esteem is low, so they target everyone with insults to feel better about themselves," she said.

Serena bathed and turned me with care and tenderness that was genuine. She made me feel accepted and worthwhile. I found out during my nursing home stay that Serena is carrying a heavy

Dear God ...

burden with her home situation and she herself is a cancer patient.

Despite all her hardships, she always has encouragement and support for me. She told me <u>never</u> to let other people's negative comments make me lose my self-worth. She said for me to stay focused on my inner light that comes from God.

I want to thank You, God, for people like Serena in this world. The care and support she showed me was essential for my health recovery. Please help lighten her burdens at home and restore her to health so she can continue to be the blessing she is to the medical community.

With Loving Gratitude,

Eva

Letters from the Nursing Home

A Letter from Sissy

Dear God,

No one ever asked me, "Are you ready for old age? Are you prepared for the changes involved in being a senior member of society?"

Frankly, with my genetic make-up and family history, I never thought I'd reach the ripe old age of eighty-one. But, as I look in the mirror every morning to view the face I present to the world, there I am, eighty-one in all of it's wrinkled glory.

I am still very young and vigorous in attitude. In my heart of hearts, I have the mental determination of a woman half my age. So I've decided not to let a number

Dear God ...

limit my life. I still have oodles of things to accomplish before I've filled my bucket (kick the bucket is way too negative).

I retired several years ago from my position as county librarian. I am now realizing I need something to look forward to in life. Something to wake up for and put a glide in my stride. After pondering for a few weeks on what would give my mind a jolt, I decided to answer an ad for tutoring students in need of improving their reading skills. Did I mention, God, that I live in a nursing home?

The social worker very kindly set up a make-shift office for me in a vacant room here.

I love to read and I love kids. Teaching has long been a calling deep in my heart. I have two students. One is seven and the other is forty-five. They're both kids as far as I'm concerned. They each come to see me at the nursing home twice weekly for hourly sessions and I love it.

It has given me a creativity push and I am continuing to be a contributing member of society. Plus, they both think I'm a hoot as well as a wonderful teacher. I wish I had known my teaching skills would be this fulfilling years ago. Each student presents a different challenge but their progress is outstanding. The nursing home art class is making their diplomas and planning a party for their graduation when classes are complete.

Dear God ...

So, God, I feel this is just the beginning of my Fill the Bucket plan. I have a few other goals up my sleeve to keep my mental acumen tweaked. Here is my list:

1. Learn to play the ukulele (a life-long wish)

2. Reconnect with an old high school chum (class of '43) via the Internet

3. Enter a poetry writing contest (haikus are my specialty)

4. Go to the local casino and play the slots (My earnings, if any, would go to the Literacy Foundation, of course)

5. Fall in love again (OK, God, this last one might be taking it a stretch but I'm still game)

At eighty-one, I still feel life is a special occasion to which I've been cordially invited. There's a heck of a lot of spunk left in this old gal. I may be wheelchair-bound, but my mind soars free. I don't want

Letters from the Nursing Home

to leave this life until I've squeezed every ounce of giving, sharing and loving out of it.

Bucket Not Quite Full,

Sissy

Dear God ...

A Letter from Helen

Dear God,

I'm feeling a little scared. I'm moving into a nursing home today. Suddenly, I have to consolidate 78 years worth of valuables, treasures and memories into a tiny room I must share with a total stranger. It almost seems impossible to me. So, what means the world to me? And what is it that I know in my heart I cannot live without?

Let's see. I'll bring this picture of my beloved parents on their wedding day—so beautiful. And here, I'll take this bundle of love letters from my husband written to me all throughout our marriage. And what about this oil painting of my two girls exquisitely created by my best friend? This will look so good over the sofa in my new home.

Letters from the Nursing Home

Finally, I must take this music box. It was given to me by my sister after my first baby died. I still find the melody so soothing when I'm sad. And the Bible that has been in my family's possession for generations. I'll keep it in my bedside stand. It's a treasure.

I'm feeling a little less frightened now, God. I realize my peace of mind is not based on where I live or how many possessions I own. What matters most is what I hold dearest to my heart.

Your Life-Long Friend,

Helen

Dear God ...

A Letter from Lottie

Dear God@HeavenAbove.com,

Believe it or not, I've decided to jump into the computer age.

My grandson bought me a brand new Dell laptop computer. I almost didn't accept it at first. I thought I was too old to learn something new at 75. But after a few lessons by a very savvy fellow senior, I'm now loving sending out e-mails to family and friends.

So, God, instead of my prayers to You each night, I'll be sending off a G-mail to You.

First of all, I'd like to thank You for all that went right in my life. My favorite nurse took care of me today and I found out that she'll be my care provider for the next two weeks.

Also, tonight's meal was just spectacular. I mean, you just can't beat ham, sweet potatoes and green beans with an ice cream sundae for dessert, can you? It's what I used to serve my family

Dear God ...

for Sunday supper when the money wasn't too tight.

But, best of all, my daughter from Cincinnati called and she's finally pregnant after trying for 12 years. You know I'm simply delighted.

But now, God, may I share the sadness in my heart?

I miss living in my own home and all the things I used to do—like planting flowers in my garden. And watching kids in the neighborhood play ball and swing on the swings. I miss the sights and sounds that I call home.

Believe it or not, God, I miss doing the laundry. Taking freshly laundered clothes off the line and folding them just so and putting them away. I miss shopping with my sister and our two-hour lunches at John's Family Restaurant. I especially miss the fried chicken and the home-made coconut cake and

Letters from the Nursing Home

slurping the best sweet tea in West Virginia on a hot summer day.

I miss going to church, my own church, where I have known most of the congregation for years. I miss lighting candles for sick friends and sitting in the last pew to finish my Rosary after Mass.

In other words, I miss my own familiar schedule and routines or having no routine at all and just flying by the seat of my pants.

I'm not ungrateful, God. I know I'm where I need to be right now. But I feel I'm missing out on my real life. I can't quite face the fact that this nursing home might be my last home before I die.

So, if You don't mind, I'll be G-mailing You each night to tell You what I am grateful for and also what I miss about the beautiful world of my past. Help me accept each day as it comes and be at peace.

Dear God ...

Your Computer Age Novice,

Lottie@PeaceValleyCtr.net

P.S. Don't worry God. I don't expect Your response by e-mail. Just send Your reply straight to my heart.

Letters from the Nursing Home

A Letter from Jenny

Dear God,

You must know by now that I love You. I begin each morning and end each night in prayer to share my thanks to You and tell You just how dear You are to me.

Dear God ...

You also know that my life has not been easy. I've lost everyone that has ever meant anything to me in this world....my parents, my siblings, my spouse, and my only child in a miscarriage. Even my best friends have gone before me. So, it's just You and me, God.

I have a lot of time to do serious and heartfelt thinking. In a nursing home, there's plenty of empty time.

But this doesn't sadden me. I've lived a very full 80 years for which I am grateful. I love to meditate and reflect on the life I've led.

I also ponder what the next life will hold for me. After all, who really knows what heaven is like? So, let me tell You about my heaven.

In my heaven, I'll see the baby I never knew. I'll marvel over her first smile, first step, first day in kindergarten. I'll hear her giggle over her first boyfriend and debate with her how old she needs to be to have her first date. I'll see her graduate from college and walk down the aisle with her life partner.

Letters from the Nursing Home

And, I'll learn from You why I was denied the delights, as well as the hardships, of knowing her in this life.

I'll see my father's smile in my heaven. And hold his hand again. And see him in the audience at my dance recitals. He'll have Miller Lites on the front porch with my husband-to-be and later walk me down the aisle to entrust him with my love. He was gone so soon from my life, God. I barely knew him since he died when I was merely 5 years old.

And there's my mother in the kitchen in my heaven—laughing at the antics of her four children and serving up the best rice pudding ever, which I requested over cake for my birthday year after year. I'll touch the softness of her beautiful face, and tell her how very much I've missed her since she died, and thank her for the innumerable sacrifices she made to provide a good education and happy life for the four of us kids. She was a marvel.

Dear God ...

In my heaven, my Rob will be my forever spouse. We'll chat about our first meeting, the day that changed everything. I'll smell his Bay Rum cologne and we'll dance the jitterbug again. We'll reminisce about our love story.

He'll tell me that my suppers were not just good but awesomely good, and how he loved to come home after work and be greeted by me and the dogs.

I'll tell him something funny and he'll laugh that Jack Lemmon laugh and call me Lucy which was his nickname for me.

Yes, this will be my heaven. Actually our heaven.

Lastly, I'd love to see my beloved dogs again, and watch them basking in the sun, and running in the park at dusk, and wagging their tails with wild abandon as they notice it is really me. I can't imagine a heaven without animals—creatures that showed us more about love than humans did.

It's been said that when we die, all we take back to God is what's in our heart. Our love. Well,

Letters from the Nursing Home

God, what's in my heart is my love for You and those I cherished in this life. Whatever heaven is, I am sure it will far surpass anything my limited human imagination can dream up. Thank You for letting me share my thoughts with You. And, as always, I love You.

Your Friend,

Jenny

Dear God ...

A Letter from Gerda

Dear God,

He died at 6:58 AM today. At first, I was frightened to be with him when he surrendered his last breath. But his peaceful face gave me courage. So, I didn't cry.

There was a spiritual peacefulness in the room I never before experienced. I felt a blessing for both of us. As I started to bathe his body for the funeral home, I realized the sacredness of this task. I was cleansing the vessel that once contained a soul now in Your presence.

When I was done, God, I spent some time reflecting on his life. He always spoke to me in a most respectful tone. He was a powerful man in both voice and stature. But there was also a

Letters from the Nursing Home

gentleness about him. I loved the way he said his daughter's name—Priscilla. It was uttered with such tenderness, with an underlying yearning to have her appear in his room. He never said her name without a smile.

I always loved the way he would settle into a comfortable chair across from the nurses' station. He had a ritual of arriving there daily at 4:30 PM, waiting for his coke and crackers. After watching the staff work and finishing his snack, he'd shuffle back to his room. He never wanted help. He prided himself in walking independently.

Dear God ...

I learned a lot about him just by being in his room each day. That he was a tri-athlete in his youth. That he enjoyed relaxing music and TV football. His granddaughter's artwork meant so much to him. He was a man of precision with a closet as perfect as any military locker. After all, he was a career military officer until his retirement.

I was glad to have had some time alone with him after his death to tell him things I wish I had told him before he died:

"Sir, you were always my favorite patient. You carried yourself with such dignity and grace. The way you walked with your head held high despite your degenerative arthritis. And I was always flattered that you remembered my name despite your severe memory loss.

I forgive you for the days you were aggressive both physically and mentally towards me. I know how devastating it was for you to lose your independence, your power,

Letters from the Nursing Home

and your strength. I think you gave up the will to live after your hip fracture when you could no longer walk without severe pain.

I thank you, sir, for dying in my presence and helping me get over my fear of death. And I salute you from my heart."

I am just at the beginning of my nursing career, God. I hope to continue to learn to work successfully with my patients and never forget the sacredness of being with someone in the last moments of their life.

Hopeful for a Fulfilling Career,

Gerda

Dear God ...

A Letter from Jack

Dear God,

What's up with all the goofy names people give nursing homes these days? Names like Hospitality Villa or Serenity Valley. Have You ever actually visited any of these places? These names are just so inappropriate and lacking in reality. Please help people wise up and come up with names more in keeping with the truth.

Letters from the Nursing Home

I came up with a few names of my own. "The Twilight Zone" where your body checks in even if your mind's checked out. Or maybe "The Bitter Pill" the place that's a little hard to swallow. Or my favorite "The Terminal Lunch". Do I even have to explain this one?

Just a few suggestions from someone who knows.

Jack

Dear God ...

A Letter from Gordon

Dear God,

I hope You don't think I'm an old fool. I'm getting married tomorrow. It has taken me 86 years to feel this way about a woman. She is charming and beautiful and though she is a younger woman at 82, we are a very good match.

The wedding is to take place in a lovely chapel in the nursing home where we reside. The staff is springing for our honeymoon at Hershey Park. We couldn't get anyone to drive us there. So, we are taking an ambulance, which at our age is probably the safest idea. Just 'cause anything can happen and this way we are prepared.

We don't plan on going on any of the dangerous rides. I have vertigo and Elsie has a bad ticker. But, we do plan to go through the Chocolate Factory and, of course, the

Dear God ...

Tunnel of Love. I might steal my first surprise kiss from her in the tunnel, because I am a very romantic man.

But, God, what I am losing sleep over is this: How are we ever going to make whoopee (may I say that to You without disrespecting You?) when we get back to the nursing home? If we don't inform the staff or our plans ahead of time, we may have a staffer walk in on us during our love fest. Then again, if we do tell someone (another embarrassing predicament), well, I can imagine a handful of nosy staffers parked outside our door with their stethoscopes dutifully pressed to the door. You know, listening for the sound of our old bones crunching!

Dear God ...

I haven't slept a wink in weeks worrying about this matter. God, it has taken me this long to find true love. I want my first night with her to be alone, just the two of us. I wrote my wedding vows last night and I hope they meet with Your approval.

"I, Gordon, take thee, Elsie, to love and cherish
From this day forth. Though we met in the twilight
Of our lives, I promise to adore you and live in the
Splender of our forever love."

I'm going to bed now. I'm exhausted with worry but at the same time thrilled with my love for my future bride. Please, Lord, help me come up with a workable answer to my dilemma.

A Soon-to-be-Married Man,

Gordon

Letters from the Nursing Home

A Letter from Freddie

Dear God,

Well, my life is in the toilet again. I was found in a pile of leaves behind my apartment building. Dressed in rags and still clutching my bottle of rotgut. As usual, I was covered in vomit. They tell me that a woman who didn't want to be identified dropped me off. Back to the local hospital and two days later to the nursing home for the third time in six months.

Everyone knows the town drunk. Nevertheless, the check in procedure begins:

- Who should they call in an emergency? The answer is always the same. I have no one. Who would own up to this scrawny stray cat?

- Who will pay? I have no money and no insurance. Every dime of my Social Security benefit check goes

Dear God ...

directly to John's Fine Liquors. I choose booze over food, work, and family every day all day long. I bleed my check dry, and then panhandle until my next payday.

I blame everything and anything possible for my drinking habit----my divorce, my deprived upbringing, my lack of education. I haven't looked in the mirror for years. Because I can't bear to face the one to blame, glaring back at me. "You did this to yourself. You miserable failure. You sorry loser."

I am lost, God. I've had some time to dry out here and think about my life. At the age of 66, death is around the corner if I don't change. But where will I get the strength and the will power?

When I was young I used to love to fish. I'd sit on the banks of the lake with friends and plan my happy future. Now when I look ahead, I see only uncertainty. A life without hope is not worth living for me.

My roommate here at the nursing home is 99 years old. And yet, he's so very full of life. Every day is an adventure for him. "A gift from God," he says.

Letters from the Nursing Home

After talking for days with him, we've sort of gotten to know each other. Surprisingly, he doesn't seem to be thrown by my horrible failings. He ends each of our chats by reaffirming----"Life is full of hope and miracles."

After I returned from my physical therapy session today, I found a letter on my bed. It said:

I've gone home today, Freddie. I once was a drunk like you. Someone took a chance on me and helped me to turn my life around. I'd like to do the same for you. Here are some things I did that can help you:

• Attend AA meetings with a friend or sponsor. I'll be yours.

• Call your daughter and make a family connection. It's worth a shot.

• Honor your body. Eat better each day. O.K., you can still have Kentucky fried chicken every Sunday.

• Walk for 30 minutes every day. Ask the healing power of nature to join you.

Dear God ...

- Honor your soul. Trust in the divine and pray often. Know that God is with you even in the worst of times—even when you're drunk.

- Bathe daily and get some new clothes, even if they are from Goodwill. Spiff yourself up. It works wonders.

- Make a list of things that bring you joy. Speak them aloud. Make them your mantra.

- Visit the pound. Walk a dog and bond with it. A dog's love is unconditional and spirit-lifting.

- Surrender your drinking to God.

- Go fishing (I love to fish, my friend) and recapture your youth.

Your Friend,

Tom

God, I'm being discharged home this coming Thursday. I think it's time to start looking in the mirror again.

Hopeful for a Full Recovery,

Freddie

Letters from the Nursing Home

Dear God ...

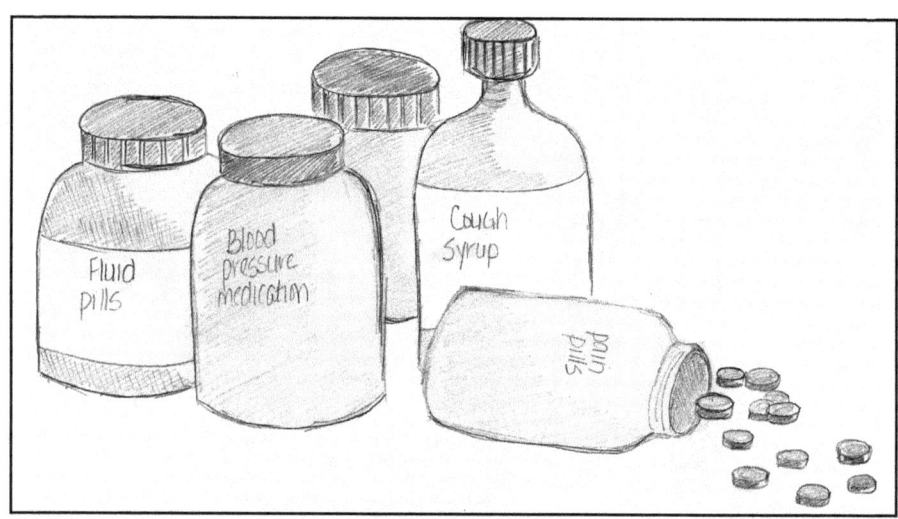

A Letter from Oscar

Dear God,

    I need some help with a big-time problem. My doctor over the years diagnosed me with 6 major health issues. For each of these issues, I have to take 2 medications to keep me healthy. If my 88 year old memory serves me correctly, 2x6 still equals 12. So I'm swallowing 12 pills daily just to stay alive.

    Now, God, You might think, "I've created these medications to keep you well, so what's your beef?"

Letters from the Nursing Home

Well, I'm gonna tell you.

The mathematics gets more complicated. Each of my 12 meds has 7 potential side effects. And some of them are real doozies. And, no, I don't remember what 12x7 equals, so I called my 9 year old granddaughter and she said it's 84.

Well, I flipped my wig. (No, I really don't wear a wig, it's just an expression we humans have.)

You already know I have an anxiety disorder, right?

Anyway, here are some of the side effects I've experienced so far: dizziness, nausea, insomnia, excessive flatulence (yes, Lord, I'm a full-blown gas bag), imbalance when walking, hives, scratchy throat, hiccups, excessive sweating, bizarre thoughts, excessive hair growth in no hair zones, hair loss where I used to have hair, rectal burning, ringing in the ears, left-sided facial drooping, blurry vision, memory loss and bankruptcy.

That's right. I'm flat broke because of my drug habit.

My question to you is: Should I go off my meds and throw caution to the wind knowing I'll be living with 6 conditions that can kill me at any time?

Dear God ...

My church has always taught me that life is precious.

How about You helping us seniors out by equipping some crackerjack genius with the smarts to create a pill with no side effects? Or better yet, one pill that cures everything. I'd be willing to pay top dollar for that gem.

At least I know my drugs aren't habit-forming. I've been on them for years!

Thanks for Listening, God,

Oscar

Letters from the Nursing Home

A Letter from Betty

Dear God,

As You know, my roommate of five years, Maggie, died last night. While it wasn't exactly a match made in Heaven (no pun intended), I miss her already. I miss her delightful British accent and the way she kept her side of the room impeccably clean and neat. I loved the smell of her floral lotions, her quirky sense of humor and even her bizarre family's visits.

What I won't miss is the way she always hogged the bathroom, her constant

Dear God ...

borrowing and losing my canes and glasses and her ear-busting snoring. So please, God, send me a new roommate that has all of Maggie's charm but none of her bad habits (especially the snoring!).

                        Thank You in Advance,
                                Betty

Letters from the Nursing Home

A Letter from Becky

Dear God,

   Momma loved her life. As far back as I can remember she was a smiling, singing, fun loving gal of West Virginia. Married to the love of her life, she made a home filled with joyful noise. Her days were spent cleaning and cooking. The smell of good eats and a welcoming home attracted the visit of many a hungry neighbor. Nothing pleased Momma more than having her kids and their friends gathered around the table, spilling stories of school news, new friendships, silly gossip and love interests. With Momma, it was always all about family.

Dear God ...

Now, our life wasn't all fun and games. When Momma raised you, you were raised right. God was #1 and we toed the line or else. After all, she was our mother as

Letters from the Nursing Home

well as our Sunday school teacher. When we acted up, she never had to get out the paddle. Her "look" of disappointment could topple a gorilla. If that failed, which it rarely did, she'd slay us with one of her "mommilies":

"Country girls know better than that," she'd admonish.

And to the boys monkeying around in the tree house: "If you fall and break your leg, don't come running to me!"

To this day I can hear her say, "A good child never disappoints the Momma."

Her education was limited but, boy, did she have street smarts. Momma could fix anything, make anything, cure anything, and, of course, love everything. Literature was her joy in life. Part of our nightly ritual was getting ready for bed and having a group reading. Some of her stories were readings of her own poetry.

Dear God ...

A poem was written for each child at their birth, when leaving home and on their wedding day. I've kept all of mine and have never been able to read one through without tears. At my birth, she wrote:

"Inspired by God, she's born to me
   With hair of silky ebony.
My love for her will fill my heart,
From this day forth til we do part."

Momma spent the past year and a half in a nursing home. Susie, Betsy and I visited every night. This was never an obligation but, instead, an honor. We came to feed, bathe, read to, sing to, comfort and just love her. The nurses always commented on how much fun we had during visiting time. Lots of laughter always poured from the room, especially when Momma's nephew, Sam, joined us.

She died a few months ago of end-stage respiratory disease. I was inspired to

Letters from the Nursing Home

write a poem to honor her shortly after her death.

For you, Momma:

"A child of God she's gone from me
To angels' arms eternally.
And though we are so far apart,
Our life of love still fills my heart."

Always and Forever,
Becky

Dear God ...

A Letter from Sally

Dear God,

   Please send me some comfort. My sadness comes from the loss of my best friend, Mia, last night. She was my constant companion, always by my side and in my heart. She understood me like no one else ever did, even my husband. Mia and I had so much in common. We liked the same TV shows, long walks, car trips and snack foods. In fact, she thought I was the greatest cook she ever had the pleasure to know. It is because of her that I have been able to adjust to life in this nursing home.

Letters from the Nursing Home

If she is with you now, give her a big hug and lots of kisses from me. She was the finest dog that ever graced this earth.

Lost Without Her,

Sally

Dear God ...

A Letter from Bonnie's Friends

Dear God,

My best friend, Bonnie, died in a nursing home a week ago today. While the funeral was sad but beautiful, what happened later that day was something I'll never forget. There was a celebration of her life and a sharing of the love and all that she meant to her dearest friends.

Bonnie loved parties. She hosted many an elegant soirée. But she also loved simple, fun-filled gatherings. Anything and everything were a cause for celebration: the first day of spring, Groundhog Day, you name it, she celebrated it. So, on the day she was laid to rest six of her closest

Letters from the Nursing Home

friends, myself included, stayed at the burial site and had a picnic. Yes, a picnic!

Just to the right of the grave site, we spread a blanket and covered it with all the foods Bonnie loved. We feasted on fried chicken (Bonnie's recipe) , potato salad, brownies and champagne. We each took time to tell the story of how Bonnie came into our lives, filled it with happiness and changed us forever. We had this party to honor her and know that she would be thrilled with how we celebrated her life rather than grieve our loss.

"And the song, from beginning to end, I found in the heart of a friend."

Dear God ...

The six of us vowed that very day to do the same for each other when the time came. Thank You, God, for bringing Bonnie into our lives. She's gone from us now, but will always remain in our hearts. Here's to female friendship, a touch of heaven's love here on earth.

                      With Love,
                Bonnie's Bosom Buddies

"And the song, from beginning to end, I found in the heart of a friend."

                      Henry Wadsworth Longfellow

Letters from the Nursing Home

A Letter About Lucy

Dear God,

It was her husband, Paul, who called with the news. Lucy's cancer had returned. Could her nursing friends come visit and buoy her spirits?

Now, when it's one of your patients with distressing health news, you know just what to do. After all, you've been a

Dear God ...

nurse for years. You assess, you care plan, you implement and discuss the results. It's second nature.

But when it's your co-worker who's ill, it's different. It's too close to home. You've spent a great portion of your life together, sharing work, seminars, tennis matches and mutual support in both good and bad days.

So what happens now, God?

What I did was to gather the troops. Five of Lucy's closest family of nurses, myself included, went on a road trip to her home in Virginia. She would not fight this cancer without her former medical posse.

Bearing our ammunition, we arrived at her home with home-made soups, baked goodies, lotions, teddy bears, angels, and prayers. Also with us were the intangibles: our common bond, empathy, humor and healing spirit.

Letters from the Nursing Home

Lucy greeted us at the door and we were not surprised. Yes, there was the bloating, the lack of hair, the obvious weight loss.

But, oh, her smiling blue eyes were just as amazing as always. The first hour was spent discussing the type of cancer, the stages, the visits to Walter Reed Medical Center, the chemo and the lack of appetite. We couldn't help but laugh at her stories of her husband's dutiful cooking experiments.

But, what Lucy really wanted to talk about was our history together.

The next three hours was about all of the things that banded us together. The five days of snow when we stayed on-site in the nursing home, worked 16-hour shifts and collapsed on a cot each night. We talked about our expanding families, shared pictures, our ideas on how nursing has changed both good and bad for the past 25

Dear God ...

years. We discussed the difficulties as well as the humorous aspects of aging.

After hours of food, talk, music, laughter and threading together the stories of our lives, we all fell silent.

There was a spectacular sunset behind our Lucy. Our time together for the day was coming to a beautiful close.

Lucy had an indomitable spirit. The day before she died, she had Paul take her out for a canoe ride. She never let cancer win.

I offer a prayer tonight, God, that Lucy is sailing along happily in heaven. Her nursing career touched and improved the lives of so many.

Her Admiring Co-workers and Friends,

Rona, Boo, Kay, April and Mel

Letters from the Nursing Home

A Letter from Bobby

Dear God,

As a child, I always looked up to my big brother. Six years my senior, braver, stronger, taller, he was a big-time hero to me. I admired his devotion to our country and was in awe when I saw him for the first time after basic training as a full-fledged Marine. He was a sight to behold.

We've always been close but cut from a different cloth. He: tough, serious, no nonsense and so much like dad with a military mindset. Me: ever the jokester, casual, outgoing with mother's softer temperament. Still, the brotherly bond was always with us. Our lives took us our separate ways, but our visits to each others' homes over the years were and still are a genuinely warm and enjoyable time.

Dear God ...

Recently, his wife, Dawn, became ill and this put a chink in his tough demeanor. But, ever the strongman, he focused on the military way. His goal was to attack the enemy, the disease, and ferret out a game plan. That's what a former gunner pilot would do.

When it became obvious his wife was losing her battle with cancer, I could feel, even though it was mainly through e-mails and phone chats, that he wouldn't mind a comforting and understanding brother by his side.

When I arrived at his home in Massachusetts, there was less of the usual bravado. His look had softened, his voice was gentler. It reminded me of when he and I visited the Vietnam Memorial for the first time.

As his fingers traced the names of his fallen comrades, he was taken to a place in the depths of his soul. Shaken, saddened, bereft with grief. But he didn't cry. A Marine endures pain. He carries on.

Letters from the Nursing Home

With his wife in a nursing home for her final days, he spent day and night by her side. Caring for her, comforting her and protecting her. I imagined our deceased mother guiding his actions and standing nearby with pride. I was lucky enough to arrive back from my home in West Virginia to support him at the time of her last day.

The nursing home staff perform a very touching routine after each of their patients die. All the nursing staff that had anything to do with Dawn's care, took part in preparing her for the funeral home. They then took a beautiful quilt, displaying the past patients' names and tenderly placed it over her body. The family and staff then walked side by side out to the waiting hearse. The quilt was then removed and put in a special room where Dawn's name would later be added.

As I walked with my brother during this sacred procession, God, I saw him for the first time ever, reduced to tears. Long, shoulder-shaking, heart-breaking sobs. As I clung to him, he whispered to me, "I guess you can see that I'm no longer that

Dear God ...

hard-assed Marine. I've changed." I whispered back, "Hard-assed, no. But Marine, yes. Semper Fi, my brother. Always faithful to your wife and kids, your parents, to me and to your duties to our country. Well done, Marine. Well done, brother."

    Still in Admiration and with Brotherly Love,

                        Bobby

Letters from the Nursing Home

Dear God ...

A Letter from Gertie

Dear God,

    We, the residents of The Cozy Nest Nursing Home, are having our first senior dance next Saturday night. Even though there is only one man for every 15 women, we are hoping for a rollicking good time, if You know what we mean. Dancing was our life when we were just young whipper-snappers. We still remember the Cha-Cha, the Swing, and, or course, the Jitterbug. Oh, what a fine time we had in those good old days!

    Would it be rude of us to inform our totally clueless 21-year old activity director that Kool and The Gang's "Get Down

Letters from the Nursing Home

on It" is not our idea of romantic, foot stomping music?

        Still Kicking, Just Not So High,
                Gertie

Dear God ...

A Letter from Ellie

Dear God,

My brother means the world to me. Today, like every day on the nursing unit, I spent my lunch hour feeding him. Yes, he's confused and dependent, and sometimes he doesn't even recognize me, but he's still my brother.

Letters from the Nursing Home

The staff often ask me, "Why do you come every day? Why don't you take a day off for yourself?"

And then I think to myself, "I wonder if they really know this man?"

He's been a sweet brother, a loving husband and father to his family, a combat pilot, and a decorated war hero. He has walked and dined with several of our Presidents. He's made crucial decisions for the safety of our country. He defended our nation at the risk of his own life and safety. He's faced hardship, prejudice, and discrimination and rose above it. He was and always will be an officer and a gentleman.

Can anyone know all this and still ask, "Why do you come every day?" I come because he needs me and I love him. He deserves all that I can do and more. I have always believed that is what family is for. He had our back and now I've got his until the very end.

A Loving Sister,

Ellie

Dear God ...

A Letter from Laura

Dear God,

The apple never fell far from the tree as far as the women in my family are concerned.

Most of us have so much in common, we could have been cloned. We all share the auburn hair, alabaster skin, athletic build, and a love for nature. None of us are musically inclined, but we love music, and sing and dance whenever we are together. We think alike, too, often finishing each others' sentences.

Unfortunately, we are linked by the breast cancer gene as well. Grandma and Mom both died of breast cancer before the age of 45. So, when my doctor said my mammo showed cancer, well, there was no real shock. It was almost expected and inevitable.

Letters from the Nursing Home

I was a senior in high school when Mom came home to die. I remember feeling claustrophobic for months—like all the air and energy was sucked out of our home. I recall my senior year as one miserable time.

So, it is for this reason, God, I have decided to spend the time I have left in a nursing home. I've been here for 3 weeks and it's working well so far. I get the hands-on care I need and my daughter is free to come and go whenever she chooses.

My daughter is living with my best friend and her family while I'm in the nursing home. They have welcomed her wholeheartedly and she will be able to stay on after I die for as long as she needs.

I don't want my daughter to have to be my caretaker. Age 16 is the time to be drooling over cute boys, shopping for clothes with her "besties", and gossiping on Facebook.

When she comes to visit me, she doesn't see it as a burden. We have quality time. She tells me all about her day, her teachers, who's dating who, and other teenage interests.

Dear God ...

The other night, she came for a visit and we watched TV, listened to music and chatted. We had such a good time, she didn't want to leave. She asked the nurse for a geri-chair and she spent the night with me. And it was her choice. I kept waking up and thanking You, God, for my decision

Letters from the Nursing Home

to give her breathing room during my illness. And for the sweet blessings of motherhood.

I gave my best friend a letter to be delivered to my child shortly after I die. I hope You approve, God.

My Dearest Daughter,

The sun has shined brighter in my life since you were born. We always had a spiritual bond and this will never be broken.

Though our time together was short, I already know that you are a child of destiny. In the years to come, you will surprise even yourself with what you are able to become and accomplish.

So don't waste even a minute of your life worrying. When the going gets tough, remember what Mimi used to say: "This, too, shall pass."

Dear God ...

Be open to guidance from those you trust as well as guidance from above.

Pray often and then just let it be.

Always dream big and follow through with hard work. Pursue what you love and live your life with passion.

Remember to pick a life partner who makes your heart sing. And it won't hurt to ask, "Would Mom approve?"

Finally, be happy with who you are, for you are God's masterpiece and my greatest achievement.

All My Love,
Mom

Letters from the Nursing Home

Thank you, God, for my life, my child and my decision to allow her freedom during my illness. And please, hurry with the cure for breast cancer. Let my child be part of the generation where breast cancer is finally history.

Peacefully Yours,

Laura

Dear God ...

A Letter from Mary

Dear God,

    She arrived today all heavenly miracle and soft skin, swaddled in her pink blanket. She smelled more delicious than sugar cookies fresh from the oven. She has her mother's fat cheeks, her grandmother's blue eyes and my long, tapered fingers and toes.

    Her mother handed her to me and I placed her on a pillow close to me in my bed. She nestled in and cooed

Letters from the Nursing Home

gently. The way she gazes at me, it's as though she's seeing me for the first time, and yet, has known me forever. I find such comfort in her presence. Slowly, she drifted off to sleep.

The very sight and sounds of her make my heart sing. I never thought I'd know this joy again, God. I'm 97 years old, in failing health and I live in a nursing home.

But today, none of this matters. My breathing is stronger. My sight is clearer. The world seems just right.

If I should die tonight, God, I'll die a happy woman. For today I spent my morning with my eldest son, his child and my first great-grandbaby, Isabella. Four generations gathered together in my room, and the love was overwhelming.

                      Thank You for a Blessed Day,

                            Mary

Dear God ...

A Letter from Sidney

Dear God,

What I wouldn't give for a thick, juicy slice of apple pie. You know, the kind my neighbor in West Virginia used to make every Sunday. She would set it on the window sill to cool on a sunny April morning. It always had the precise amount of cinnamon and nutmeg and an aroma that still has my taste buds firing up just thinking about it.

I also recall a top-of-the-line baker at a hole-in-the-wall Greek restaurant I used to visit when I had the dough. Their apple pie must have been 10 inches high with apples spilling over the sides of a sturdy aluminum pan. I'd buy the whole pie and polish it off with my buddies. You had to pay $1.25 extra for the pan, but you got the money refunded when you returned the pan.

Letters from the Nursing Home

I'm sure the head cook in this nursing home is not even vaguely acquainted with the term home-made. Out of the box and cheap as possible is all she knows.

I don't think it's asking too much, God, to send me a bit of pie that would remind me of the old days. When I had choices and little things to look forward to. Just pie, God. And maybe a dollop of creamy vanilla ice cream on the side. And to top it off, a piping hot cup of Joe. A friend to visit and share it with wouldn't be a bad idea either.

How about it, God? My taste buds are waiting.

Sidney

Dear God ...

A Letter from Mickey

Dear God,

    Do You ever get depressed? I'm afraid some days You must with what goes on in the world. Crime, illness, war, pestilence. These must be disheartening even for You. So, on the chance that today is a total bummer for You, I've come up with a list of things I know You've done just right. I could go on and on forever, but here are a few things You can pat Yourself on the back for.

Letters from the Nursing Home

Wildflowers
Hummingbirds
Chocolate
Babies' skin
Lightning
Peace
Johnny Mathis music
Waves at the beach
Fluffy dogs
Laughter
Marriage
Pinot Grigio wine
Clouds
Gentle rain
Milkshakes
Acts of kindness
Pasta
Flannel sheets
Miracles
Did I mention chocolate? You did really good there!
Baseball
Mountains
Peace
Family

Dear God ...

Justice
First love
True love
Eternal love
Your divine love

You're the Best, My Friend,

Mickey

Hope Valley Nursing Home

Newton, New Jersey

Letters from the Nursing Home

A Letter from Sharon

Dear God,

My dear Dad passed away at the nearby nursing home two weeks ago today. Several of the nurses wrote beautiful notes of condolence which are a comfort to me. They mentioned how they were all tickled by the way Dad could never remember to use the call bell properly. He just whistled when he needed assistance. They said it would have been annoying if he hadn't had a unique and beautiful way to whistle. It had a songbird quality that made it endearing. It was a sound that filled our home all my life and it's one of the things I'll remember always.

I have so many fond recollection of my Dad. He always wore Old Spice which I found a clean and refreshing scent. As a child, I loved to kiss him

Dear God ...

just to capture the smell on my clothes. That way, a part of him was with me all day at school. He also had such a beautiful, genuine smile. And, I loved the way he continued to flirt with Mom, even after 55 years together.

I was listening to The Andy Griffith Show last night and I started to cry. It reminded me of Dad's love of whistling. He won many a contest for his whistling skills. When we were youngsters, every kid on the block knew it was supper time because of Dad. He even had a special whistling sound to bring the dogs home.

Letters from the Nursing Home

After supper each evening, we girls were expected to clean up and set the table for the next day. It was always part of our chores. But, if we got clever and started to whistle, Dad would leave whatever he was working on, even if he was grading his students' papers, grab a towel, and start whistling songs with us. We used this clever ploy so many times to enlist his help with the dishes. There was always a sense of joy when he joined us even though I'm sure he knew what we were up to.

His funeral was both a sad and a joyous occasion. So many friends and neighbors came to celebrate a good man of value. Everyone had a wonderful story to share about him.

My 8-year old was particularly devastated by "Pop-Pop's" death. At the funeral home, he knelt before his body and wept. I saw him slip something into his grand-father's pocket. Of course, it was a whistle. "I'm hoping I'll hear it tonight and know he's home with Jesus," was his tearful explanation.

Dear God ...

Later that night, I heard the low, moaning whistle of a train passing through the nearby town. As all my memories flooded back, I prayed: All praise and thanks to You, God, for a wonderful father. And thanks for every note with which he filled our hearts.

A Loving Daughter,
Sharon

Letters from the Nursing Home

A Letter from Virginia

Dear God,

I have 10 important things to share with You:

1. I love You.
2. I love my five children with all of my heart and soul.
3. I've been told that I have a beautiful smile and I thank You for it.
4. Music and good books move me spiritually and emotionally.
5. I love to laugh (in fact, I'm a giggler).
6. I enjoy good food. (I guess You can tell by my hefty size)
7. I enjoy learning new things every day.
8. The computer age has captured my curiosity and my intellect. It has opened up a whole new world for me.

Dear God ...

9. I love pretty flowers, fragrant perfumes and fine wines.

10. I have multiple sclerosis. I suffer with the dependency and isolation it has imposed on me.

Please, God, let people see that I am so much more than my disease. Though I am in a wheelchair and have limited movement, my mind is the same and I still love life and people. Let people not count me out because of my disease.

Still Hopeful for a Full Life,

Virginia

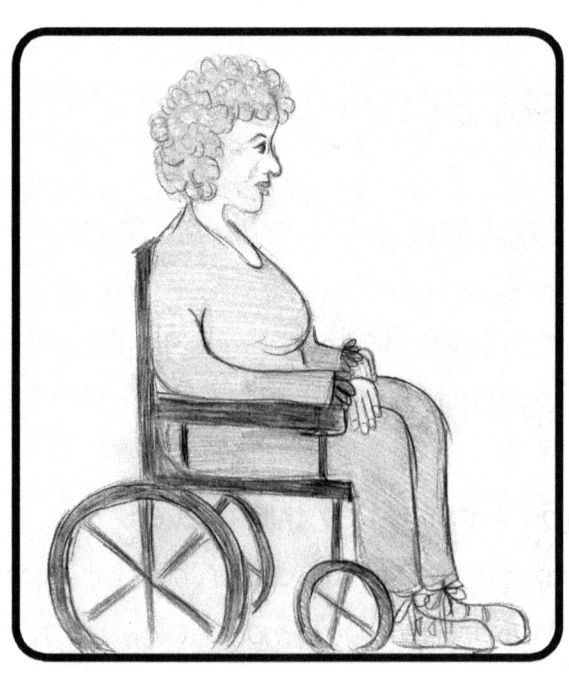

Letters from the Nursing Home

A Letter from Julie

My Dearest Lord,

As You know, I'm married one year today.

I love being 24 and in love with my husband. But when I get philosophical about life, I often think, what makes love endure? How do I know if we have the kind of relationship that can weather life's storms?

Recently, I joined the Outreach to the Elderly Program at my church. This was done to give back some of the blessings life has bestowed on me. At a local nursing home I visit an elderly blind woman and read to her from the Bible every Thursday.

Dear God ...

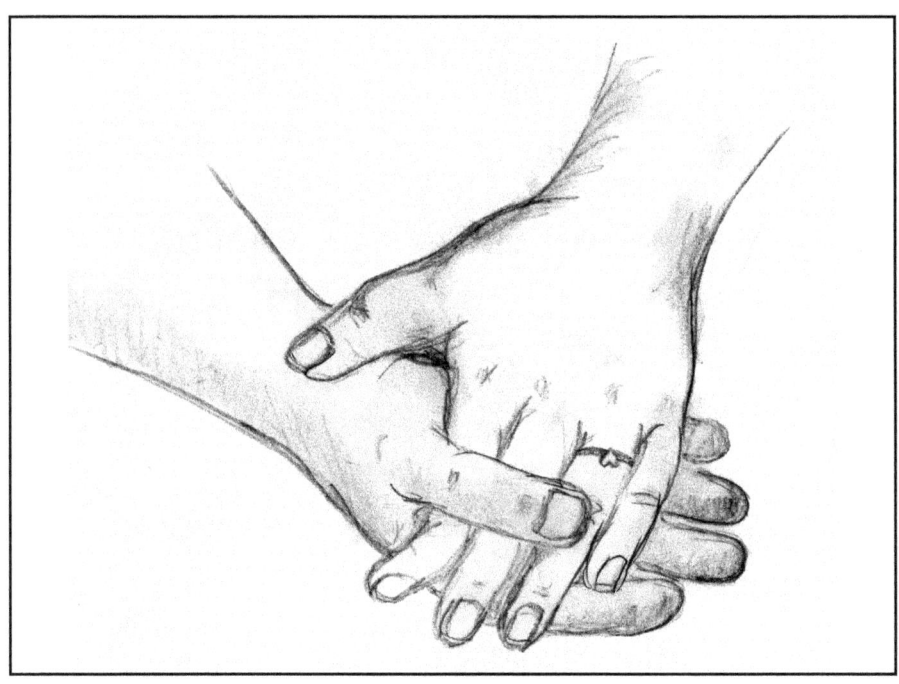

While I find this fulfilling, I've also noticed a married couple who reside there and they've touched my heart.

Last week, while at the nursing home, I peeked in a doorway that was partly ajar. I saw the married couple in separate beds. I heard the woman question softly, "Joe, are you there?" Then I saw his hand slide slowly through his bed rail to meet her hand. She wrapped her fingers around his fist and they promptly fell asleep.

Letters from the Nursing Home

What amazed me was that the man was snoring so loudly, I was sure he was asleep and didn't hear her call his name. It was like a pure love reflex to reach for her and hold hands.

When the aide in the room saw my look of surprise, she said, "Oh, sweetie, this is their daily nap time ritual. She calls for her Joe and they hold hands as they sleep. They've done this daily for the three years I have known them. They hold hands in the lunch room, at activities, during meals and just about everywhere they go. And she always calls him 'my Joe' when she refers to him. He stopped talking about six months ago after a major stroke. Touch is their best way of communicating. By the way, her name is Ida Mae, and they would love a visit from you if you ever have time."

Last week after my weekly Bible reading, I looked into Joe and Ida Mae's room. Joe's bed was empty.

Dear God ...

The aide saw my questioning expression and said "Joe died three days ago from pneumonia."

Dear Lord, I never did get to know Ida Mae and Joe as a couple, but their hand-holding ritual spoke volumes to me.

My prayer tonight is two-fold. First, please give Ida Mae comfort in the loss of her life-long love. Also, let my husband and I have what they experienced throughout their life: a strong and enduring love story.

Your Newly Wed Believer,
Julie

Dear God ...

A Letter from Arianne

Dear God,

Dad's sound asleep in his bed. Despite his nurse's attempt to keep him properly positioned, his body is twisted in a tight ball. He looks so uncomfortable. There's an underlying anguish present that breaks my heart. Dad can no longer speak. A feeding tube provides his nourishment 24 hours a day. A mere shadow of his former self, he's lost 45 lbs. He is dependent on the nursing staff for his every need. Dad has Alzheimer's disease and he is in the end stage now.

I have a routine when I visit him. I kiss him and tell him I love him. I brush his hair and rub lotion on his dry, fragile skin. Then there's my report on what's going on at home with my son. All the while, Dad watches me. I look for the

Dear God ...

faintest glimmer of recognition and I think, and pray, he somehow knows it's me. Hope he feels my love. I try to move beyond the profound sadness of his current health circumstances and reflect on the past: the man he was, the pillar of strength he was to our family and what he has always meant to us.

Sundays are my special days with Dad, God. I like to sit near him and reminisce about my childhood times with him. I have such beautiful memories. Dad took me to my first Girl Scout father-daughter dance. He had 2 left feet but we danced every dance and laughed all night. Afterwards, we stopped at a local Dairy Queen and had enormous banana splits. It's still like it happened yesterday in my mind.

Dad loved the fact that I was a tomboy as a child. He bought me my first baseball glove, Lionel train set, tool kit and he helped me build my own tree house. He was tickled by the fact that I could throw a baseball or football better and further than both my older brothers. I still have Dad's baseball

Dear God ...

glove and keep it in a special place with other treasures. Fond memories are such a special gift.

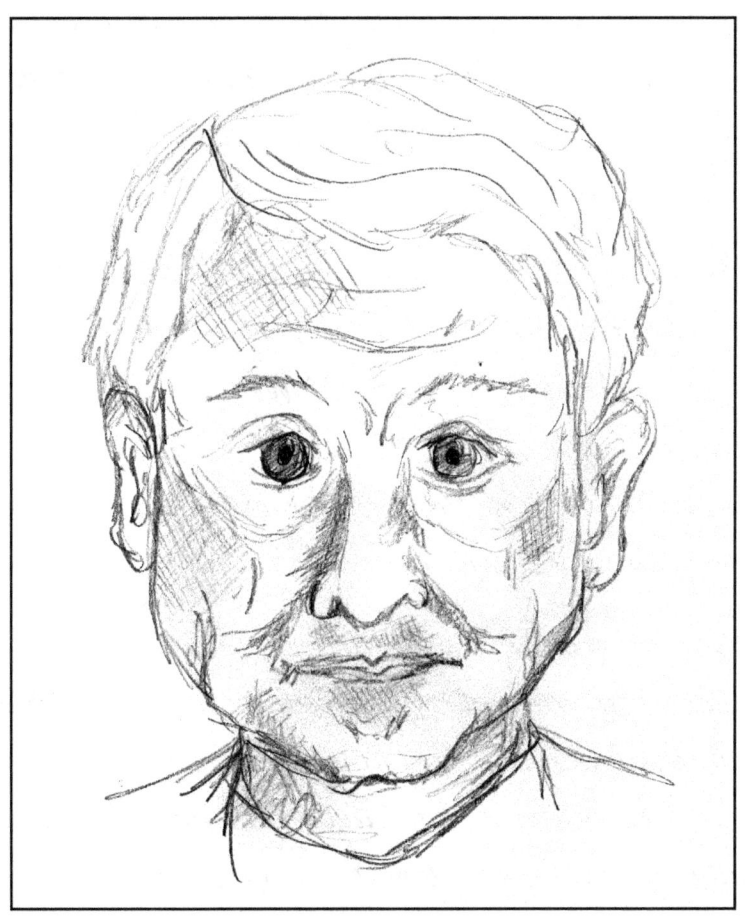

Dad loved summertime. He always had a glowing tan from working outdoors. He lived for the family's two-week vacation at the Jersey shore. Though slender in frame, he had powerful shoulders and could swim for hours. He made sure

Dear God ...

each of his children could swim as well. As young children, he would take us down to the boardwalk before bedtime for a special treat of root beers and cinnamon toast. To this day, I can't drink a root beer or smell anything with cinnamon in it without feeling Dad with me.

There is a heavy weight on my soul, God, to see my father this diminished in body and spirit. How much longer must he suffer? Why do worthy and honorable people suffer? Does he benefit at all from my visits? Dad's suffering has surely been a test of my endurance and faith.

With his Alzheimer's disease, I'm already experiencing what it will mean to lose my father. No more supportive, loving phone calls. No more sage advice when crucial decisions must be made. No more strong shoulders to cling to in good and bad times. I have tears in my eyes thinking about it.

Despite what this disease has taken, dad's many traits will live on in his family. My son is the image of his grandfather with his jet black

Dear God ...

hair, dimples and quick wit. This is a source of great comfort to me. Dad's athletic abilities and analytical mind lives on in me. If ever there was a chip off the old block that would be me. And I couldn't be prouder. He's always been my hero.

I end each visit with Dad the same way, God. I hold his hand and tell him, "Dad, you are not alone in these final days. I promise to be by your side, to pray for you, and comfort you. I promise to follow your example and to live my life with integrity. You are the best father a woman could have. You mean everything to me. Mom's been missing you for a long, long time. It's time to join her now. Your work is done. Don't ever be afraid that I will forget you. As long as I live, you will be in my heart."

Thanks for letting me share my burdened heart with You, God. You are my favorite support buddy. I hope to see You in heaven someday.

Dad's Loving Daughter,

Arianne

Dear God ...

A Letter from Jeff

Dear God,

I've never dared say much to You because, frankly, You know all, always have, always will. But now I'm going to tell You anyway about our (Anne and Jeff's) romance, which You must already know about as well as the gazillion other romances that have occurred since Adam and Eve got together in the Garden of Eden.

If this bores You, shut me up----a lightning bolt would do it, or You could send Gabriel with his terrible swift sword. So here goes.

Now I've got to admit that the very first step in our romance was lustily sexual. Hope this doesn't shock or even surprise You. After all, You created us, made us the way we are.

Letters from the Nursing Home

We were 17 years old, or nearly, when love struck.

The Junior Prom loomed. We were in the country high school decorating the gym. There was sweet music playing. My old girl friend had gone off with a 27-year-old Army Air Force pilot (It was World War II and things moved pretty fast then.), and Anne's sometime boyfriend had somehow neglected or forgotten to ask her early on to the prom.

Anne, wearing nicely fitted white slacks, climbed a ladder to put up a banner; I followed close, very close, behind to help.

The view right in front of my eyes was, well----never mind. I'm sure You know what a slim, young female's derriere looks like in or out of slacks. After all You formed these lovely creatures out of Adam's rib, and that very much included what the slacks in front of me covered.

The long and short of it: right then and there I asked her to go to the prom. Whether it was my heavy breathing at the moment, the hungry

137

Dear God ...

look on my face when she glanced down at me, or impatience with her lackadaisical boyfriend...Anne said YES!

Oh, the wonder of it!

May 8, 1943, my 17th birthday. I brought her gardenias (they became her favorite flowers).

The prom band played "Embraceable You"...it became our song.

Afterward in the sweet darkness behind the school we kissed, several times---a pretty racy first date thing in those days.

Our romance picked up speed. Dates every weekend. Holding hands in the school hallways. Touching knees under the library table. Each date, each touch deepened our love, our desire for each other.

As graduation approached, Anne joined the U.S. Nurse Cadet Corps and I enlisted in the Navy. We wanted to get married, but her Dad said "no" adding, "What if he doesn't come back from the war?"

Letters from the Nursing Home

We wrote to each other every day. The war ended. GIs raced home, got married, had babies.

We had seven, thereby fulfilling Your divine admonition to go forth and populate the earth. And we have 15 grandchildren, four great-grandchildren. Proud? You betcha!

We traveled the world, lived in France, The Congo, Zambia, Laos, Ethiopia, Kenya.

Dear God ...

We kept our children with us even in risky places until they went off to college. We moved our household 22 times. Our kids are wonderful, beautiful, adaptable.

We saw the great cities and sights of Europe, the Pyramids, the rain forests of Africa, the temples of Southeast Asia.

You know very well what we were doing; most of my work was secret. But not to You, of course.

We danced the sinuous Lan Zang under a full moon in the King's Palace in Vientiane, patted wild white rhinos in Africa, gazed on the ancient Machu Picchu, swam with young sea lions in the Galapagos, tented across the United States, hosted a hippo barbecue beside the Congo River, listened to Buddhist monks chant through the warm nights in Southeast Asia, heard lions roar in the outskirts of Lusaka, and danced, danced, danced.

It would take a millennium to tell it all, and I don't have the time. But You know it anyway.

Anne got a degree with honors in archeology, worked in museums in Addis Ababa and Nairobi,

Letters from the Nursing Home

did good work in Zambia and Laos among the local peoples. She made quilts for each of our children. After retirement from the government, I wrote novels...not very profitable ones I'm afraid. I frankly could use a little help here.

Tragedy struck in Paris---our April died of leukemia on her third birthday. If You and I ever come face-to-face, I will ask You why. We still grieve after all these years; we hope and pray that April waits for us when we get to the hereafter.

And that may be fairly soon. Anne is critically ill now.

We are 86, married 66 years, lovers almost 70 years. The excitement, the thrill of our flesh together, of each kiss, each embrace never fades. We are still 17-year old lovers in our memories and our hearts.

Anne created a book of family stories and photos in our late middle age. Her introduction: "Once upon a time a girl and a boy fell in love. All they wanted to do was get married, have a lot of children, and see the world. And So They Did."

Dear God ...

Those last four words became the title of the book. And that just about says it all.

Thank You, God, for giving us life, love, children, happiness, exciting lives. It all went by so very fast. I wish we could do it all over again.

Jeff

Letters from the Nursing Home

Pearls of Wisdom from the Nursing Home

- Anywhere there is peace, joy, and contentment can be called home.

- Start each day with a prayer. Trust in God and let the rest of the day take care of itself.

- You're never too old to share a smile, make a new friend, or fall in love

- Always be gentle with your words, for everyone you meet is fighting the good fight, just as you are.

- Never give up. There might be a miracle right around the corner.

- Meditate when you are lonely. It's a good way to bathe yourself in peace.

- On your saddest days, just look out the window. Watch the birds who are poetry in motion and know there is a God.

Dear God ...

- Don't forget to nourish your soul every day. Read a book. Listen to music. Look through your family pictures. Send a love letter to your child. Your spirit will soar.

- See each new day as an opportunity to live fully and love with all your heart.

- Count your blessings not your wrinkles, gray hairs, or problems

- Wish upon a star tonight and pray, above all, for world peace.

Letters from the Nursing Home

*Top Ten Things
My Nursing Training Never Prepared Me For
In My Long-Term Nursing Career*

1) <u>Death</u>: I never learned in school that I would be the one calling the family after their loved one passed away. I always thought it would be the doctor's role. It's been a hard-earned learning process. All I can say is it gets better with time and experience, but it's never an easy task.

2) <u>Time Management for Medication Passing</u>: My first few weeks on the job I thought: I have to pass meds to how many people in what length of time? Seriously? Seriously?? It gets faster but it's always a race with the clock and I don't always win.

3) <u>Taking a Lunch Break</u>: With tons of work, documentation on computer, dealing with family concerns and learning new skills, where, oh where, does the lunch break fit in? Sometimes it doesn't.

4) <u>Taking a Potty Break</u>: This may seem ridiculous, but it is <u>so</u> hard to squeeze in a potty break while on the job. I often think it would be easier to have a foley catheter inserted and drag around a drainage bag strapped to my leg so I don't have to worry about the bathroom time problem.

5) <u>Other Jobs as They Arise</u>: I thought I went to school to be a nurse. I never expected to be a moving company, mechanic, plumber, psychiatrist, referee, interior decorator, and mind reader. Nurses wear many hats and we just have to go with the flow.

6) <u>Stress</u>: The turnover in long-term care nursing is mind-blowing. We just lost our newest hire after two months. She went back to working in the emergency room. "Not as stressful" she explained. I rely on my own stress relievers while on the job and draw on them in time of need. I usually stop what I'm doing, take several mindful breaths then go on with my work.

7) <u>Doctor's Handwriting</u>: Please, if there is a course offered anytime, anywhere, there are nurses like myself who will attend it if it will help us get a better handle on how to decipher doctors' notes and orders.

Letters from the Nursing Home

8) <u>Setting Priorities:</u> This is another skill that is only acquired over time. Every nurse has an occasional melt-down when the job load is overwhelming. It's best to have a buddy at work who can talk you through it. A big hug helps. So does chocolate.

9) <u>The Computer:</u> I was taught that the computer will save me time. This is not always the case. There are days when the computer misbehaves and I wish it would just blow up.

10) <u>Loving the Job</u>: No instructor in nursing can prepare you for the day when you realize you were <u>meant</u> to be a nurse. The day when you know in your heart that you truly helped someone improve their health and have a better life, or die without pain and with dignity. This comes with a deep satisfaction that is undeniable. It's why we carry on.

Nicole

Dear God ...

Gift Ideas for Nursing Home Residents

Gifts are presents from the heart to express our love, appreciation and joy in knowing someone special. A gift presented on special occasions or for no reason at all except to show our love is a delight for both the giver and the receiver. Here are some gift ideas especially suited for nursing home residents. Surprise someone today in a nursing home and watch your own happiness blossom.

- Deliver and read mail to the residents.

- Have a personalized grooming session. Do the resident's nails and hairdo if you are talented in those skills.

- Bring in a soft and comfy gift such as a lap robe, bed jacket, hand-made quilt for the bed or nonskid socks.

- Provide videos on topics that are of interest to your particular resident. Do you travel and have videos? Offer to do an activity showing where you've been. Lead a discussion group afterwards.

- Pet visits. Have your church group arrange scheduled visits to the nursing home with dogs, rabbits, birds and oth-

Letters from the Nursing Home

er animals of interest. Clear this with the nursing home first.

- Bring music and dance. Can you play at instrument? Do you dance or know of a child or adult dance studio that would like to showcase their talents? Bring them to the NH to entertain the residents.

- Help with inside activities common on the NH unit. Read letters to the visually impaired, call out Bingo numbers, read menus and help with food selections, help decorate bulletin boards, help new residents set up and decorate their rooms. The activity director will think you are an angel.

- Provide home-made goodies (once they are cleared by the nursing staff based on dietary restrictions). Some ideas that are usually a big hit are ice cream socials, cookies and candies, puddings, soups and breads i.e. banana bread.

-

- Bring in old clothing still in good condition for residents without family or monetary resources.

- Offer your time in good weather days to provide outdoor wheelchair rides for nature "walks", bird watching and other fresh air activities.

- Lead a craft making activity. Organize a "create your own

Dear God ...

card" group and help them send a message to someone they love.

- Help set up a pen-pal group with residents from other nursing homes.

- Give the gift of yourself and your time. Spread the love. Give some hugs. Hold some hands. Pray with someone. Be the intent listener. Visit weekly and let someone know they are not alone. You'll be blessed beyond measure.

Dear God ...

Favorite Recipes from the Nursing Home Staff

You might be asking yourself: "Where do <u>recipes</u> fit in in a book of letters to God from the nursing home "? And this would be a legitimate question. Well, let's just say food is a delicious way to thank yourself when you are dog tired after putting in a long day of nursing work. Nurses work hard. Sometimes we don't get to eat lunch or supper at all while on duty. We carry on until the job is done. But our stomachs are screaming---"Nourish me, you fool!" We fantasize about a day when we have a full 30 minutes to sit and eat a satisfying meal. Good food with someone you work shoulder to shoulder with all day is both a joy and a blessing. Plus, home-made food is a wonderful gift to bring in for a nursing home resident's enjoyment. So there… that's where the recipes come in.

Here are just a few of my favorite recipes shared by nursing home staffers over the years. Most of them are not particularly healthy, but what's the fun in that anyway? Who cares if Doctor Oz or Michele Obama approve? Live dangerously. Life is short.

Letters from the Nursing Home

This first recipe was given to me by my husband's football friend back in the 80s. I've made it innumerable times and it has never failed me. I made it for a Christmas party at my old nursing job on a day when we actually got to sit down for an hour during the shift to eat. Unheard of! The administrator must have just received his sizeable Christmas bonus. The food was a big hit and the recipe has been shared and enjoyed by many over the years.

Missy and Ali's Chicken and Wine in Mushroom Sauce

Ingredients:

½ cup of vegetable oil
6-8 washed, skinned and boned chicken breasts
½ cup flour mixed with ½ cup of seasoned bread crumbs
½ tsp salt and ¼ tsp of pepper
2 beaten eggs
1 package of freshly sliced mushrooms
¾ cup of white wine
¾ cup of chicken broth

Directions:

Heat oil in a large, deep frying pan. Combine flour, bread crumbs salt and pepper.

Dredge chicken breasts in egg, and then flour and bread crumb mixture. Cook in hot oil for 10 minutes on each side until nicely browned. Remove from pan. Put in mushrooms and sauté until browned. Re-add chicken to pan. Pour in wine

Dear God ...

and chicken broth and cover. Cook another 15-20 minutes until chicken is fork tender.

Don't let liquids boil away. If necessary add more broth and wine to have enough liquids for the sauce. Thicken liquids with cornstarch if necessary. Serve with pasta and a vegetable or salad.

Prepare to be complimented over your delicious meal.

My Director of Nursing at my last job made this dessert for a pot luck get-together. It was a huge hit since we were all chocoholics. I recommend eating the dessert late in the day when you're nearly ready to leave work. It will give you a sugar rush of monumental proportions. Unfortunately, when the rush is over, you'll need to be somewhere you can nap for 30 minutes. Or 2 hours. Trust me on this. It's called Death by Chocolate and it's lethally good.

Kay's Death by Chocolate Cake

Ingredients:

1 box of chocolate or German chocolate cake mix
1 can of sweetened condensed milk
¾ jar of chocolate or caramel topping
1 container of Cool Whip
2-3 Heath bars, crunched

Letters from the Nursing Home

Directions:

Bake cake as directed on the box. Let it cool. Poke holes in the cake. Pour sweetened condensed milk over the cake. Let this settle in a bit.

Pour warmed chocolate or caramel sauce over the top. Let it cool.

Top with Cool Whip. Crumble Heath bars and put on top of the Cool Whip. Enjoy.

Don't forget to watch out for the sugar rush and later, the energy wipeout. Or, just have another piece or two to keep you going. Don't worry about the calories involved. Worrying will kill the sugar high!

Here's a tasty chicken treat that's good as a dip with chips. The night staff often invite me to their break-time food get-togethers when I'm finally finished my work from the earlier shift. And boy, am I glad to be invited! They can put out quite a spread. I've asked for this recipe to make at home and my husband loves it. He says it goes very well with hockey, baseball and football games, so that means it is good all year long. If you make it at work, I recommend doubling or tripling the recipe. You don't want anyone slitting your tires 'cause they never even got a taste of it, do you? Barb's not just a good cook. She's the reliable, go-to nurse for anything you need to know in nursing. A living, breathing encyclopedia of medical know how.

Dear God ...

Barb's Taco Chicken Dip

Ingredients:

8 oz of cream cheese softened
1 large can of chicken (white meat)
½ c of hot buffalo sauce
½ c of ranch dressing
2 c of sharp cheddar cheese
Lg bag of tortilla chips or scoop chips

Directions:

Spread cream cheese in an ungreased 1 quart baking dish. Layer in the chicken, buffalo wing sauce and ranch dressing. Sprinkle with cheddar cheese.

Bake in 350 degree over for 20-25 minutes until cheese if melted.

Serve warm with chips. Listen for the oohs and aahs.

Here's another sweet treat for you. This comes from Deb, a new nurse who is sure to be a nurse superstar before long. She's gifted in so many ways. She's already aware that chocolate is one of the four basic food groups. Isn't she a wiz? You might just need a nap after this recipe, too. The sugar rush strikes again!

Letters from the Nursing Home

Chocolate Pecan Pie

Ingredients:

8 squares of semi-sweet baking chocolate
1 refrigerated pie crust
2 Tbsp butter
3 eggs, slightly beaten
¼ cup of firmly packed light brown sugar
1 cup of corn syrup
1 Tsp of vanilla
1 ½ Cups of pecan halves

Directions:

Heat oven to 350 degrees.

Coarsely chop 4 squares of chocolate and set aside

Line 9" pie plate with pie crust per directions

Microwave remaining 4 squares of chocolate and butter until butter is melted. Brush crust with small amount of beaten egg. Stir sugar, corn syrup, eggs and vanilla into chocolate mixture until well blended. Stir in pecans and chopped chocolate.

Pour into crust.

Bake 55 minutes or until knife inserted 2 inches from edge comes out clean. Enjoy, enjoy, enjoy!

Dear God ...

This recipe was given to me by the dietician at my old job. Nancy is a very organized cook. She always has everything written out on adorable recipe cards. Her menu is planned days in advance and she shops early so she has everything she needs on hand. Don't you just hate people like that?

Anyway, she's a wonderful cook and shared this fab dish which has been taste-tested and wins rave reviews.

Nancy's Family Time Spaghetti Sauce

Ingredients:

4 Tsp of olive oil
1 lb. sweet Italian sausage, cut up
2/3 lb. hot Italian sausage, cut up
½ lb. ground beef
½ lb. ground pork
½ cups diced yellow onions
5 cloves of garlic, minced
3 cans (35 oz. each) Italian plum tomatoes
¾ cups tomato paste
½ cup red wine
1 cup chopped Italian parsley
1 Tbsp oregano
1 ½ Tsp. of black pepper
Salt to taste
Pinch of hot red pepper flakes
Pinch of granulated sugar
Grated zest of 2 lemons

Letters from the Nursing Home

Directions:

Heat 2 Tbsp olive oil in a skillet. Brown the sausage in small batches

Remove to a heavy casserole. Drain all but 3 Tbsp of the grease. Brown ground beef and pork and remove to casserole.

Add onions and half the garlic to the skillet Cook over medium heat 5 minutes, stirring. Add to meat in casserole.

To casserole, add plum tomatoes (with juice), tomato paste, wine, ½ cup parsley, remaining olive oil, oregano, pepper, salt, pepper flakes, sugar and half the lemon zest.

Bring the sauce to a boil and reduce heat. Simmer partially covered, over low heat for 2 ½ hours. Stir occasionally so sauce doesn't stick to casserole.

After 2½ hours, add remaining garlic, parsley and lemon zest. Stir well and cook an additional hour, stirring occasionally. Adjust seasoning to your taste and serve over your favorite pasta.

Yield: 4 Quarts

After you cook and enjoy eating this dish ask someone else to do the dishes. You're the cook, hence, you're the Queen. And the Queen <u>never</u> has to do the dishes. (These are <u>my</u> rules, not Nancy's. Nancy probably cleans up as she works and her kitchen is always spotless. I really <u>do</u> hate her!)

Dear God …

The next is my mother's rice pudding recipe. I think she stole it from Aunt Loretta or Aunt Dolores and claimed it as her own. Who cares? It's sooooo delicious. As children on our birthdays, my siblings and I never wanted cake. No siree. We wanted mom (nick-named Tootsie when we could get away with it) to make her famous rice pudding. I can still see my mother carrying the big bowl of pudding with the candles wobbling to and fro all afire. Some memories are just so fine. Miss you, mom.

Tootsie's Rice Pudding

Ingredients:

4 eggs
1 cup of sugar
½ Tsp of salt
4 cups of milk, scalded
1 tsp of vanilla
2 cups of cooked rice
Nutmeg, cinnamon and sugar

Directions:

Heat oven to 350 degrees. Beat eggs, sugar and salt slightly to mix.

Stir in scalded milk very slowly so you don't cook the egg mixture. Add vanilla and cooked rice. Pour into a large baking dish. Sprinkle with nutmeg, cinnamon and some sugar. Set in a pan of water at least 1 ½ inches deep. Bake for 60-65 minutes.

Letters from the Nursing Home

You may have to play around with the time until it is fully baked and sets. (This is a very good dessert to bring to a nursing home resident. It's easy to eat and digest and smells heavenly. Just be sure to ask the nurse if the patient has any restrictions on their diet first.)

There's nothing better than soup on a cold winter evening. Nicole provided this recipe. How she has time to cook, I'll never know. She has a house full of kids and a full-time nursing job and she's a budding artist. She's always thinking of ways to get the staff better organized at work, and I swear sometimes I see smoke pouring out of the top of her head from her brain in constant over-drive. After eating this soup you'll surely think—Yes, soup is good food. And great brain food too.

Rose Family Red Soup

Directions: Dice three large potatoes. Place in large pot and cook until potatoes are soft but not mushy. Add one can of tomato paste.

Add one small bag of frozen mixed vegetables. Add one minced garlic and one finely chopped onion. Next, add one can of corned beef and cabbage. Season with salt and pepper to taste. Cook on medium heat for ½ hour, then serve. Best served with corn bread.

Dear God ...

Teal and Heather are two young nurses who look like food isn't very important to them. Nothing could be more untrue. They both eat like horses, but remain paper thin waifs. The rest of the staff would hate them if they weren't so sweet and helpful while on duty. Maybe they dance off the extra calories from their ginormous appetites? You should see their "fish dance" and the "rodeo round-up dance". Not likely to get fat expending that kind of energy. Here are their cookie recipes. Don't forget to dance if you over-indulge!

Heather's Zucchini Drop Cookies

Ingredients:

1 c. shredded zucchini
½ c. Crisco
1 egg
1 c. sugar
1 tsp. baking soda
2 c. flour
½ tsp. nutmeg
½ tsp. salt
½ tsp. cloves
1 tsp. cinnamon
Optional: walnuts and raisins

Directions:

Beat zucchini, soda, sugar, and Crisco together

Add egg; beat; add flour, spices and optional.

Beat. Drop by rounded tbsp. onto cookie sheet.

Bake at 375 for 12-14 minutes.

Eat to your heart's content, then dance the Fish Dance or other energetic dance that you choose.

Teal's Pumpkin Gems

Cookie

Ingredients:

1 box of yellow cake mix
1 tsp. baking soda
3 eggs
2 tsp. cinnamon
½ c. oil
1 (20 oz.) can of pumpkin

Directions:

Preheat oven to 350. Blend together cake mix, eggs, oil, baking soda, cinnamon and pumpkin. Fill paper lined mini-muffin pans 2/3 full. Bake for 15 minutes. Cool, then frost.

Frosting

Ingredients:

3 oz of cream cheese, softened
½ tsp. vanilla
¾ c. butter, softened
1 T. milk
2 c. powdered sugar

Directions:

Cream together butter and cream cheese. Beat in vanilla and milk. Gradually add powdered sugar until frosting is the desired consistency. Eat these cookies like there's no tomorrow, but don't forget to dance!

This final recipe is another sweet treat. It is our other nurse Deb's cake recipe, handed down through the generations. Deb lost her mom a year ago and it was a sudden death that was very hard to bear. She was never able to make this cake without her mom's help. Baking it alone it always fell flat as a pancake. While it might still be delicious, who wants to serve up a sloppy cake?

Deb's first attempt to make this cake solo took place this past Thanksgiving. She looked to the heavens prior to starting the recipe and prayed mom would be by her side during the baking process. She mixed the ingredients, just like mom would, and it smelled so delicious and familiar while baking. But the true test was in the first cut. She was shaking so badly her husband took

Letters from the Nursing Home

the knife from her hand and sliced it for her. Mom would be so proud---the cake was perfection!

Grammy's Pound Cake

Ingredients:

3 sticks of softened butter
3 cups of granulated sugar
6 eggs
1 cup of milk
½ tsp of baking powder
3 cups of flour
1 tsp of lemon or orange extract

Directions:

Cream butter and sugar well. Add eggs one at a time. Mix well after each egg. Add milk then dry ingredients last. Put mix in a Bundt pan and place it in a cold oven. Then turn the oven on to 325 degrees. Bake for approx. 1 ½ hours, maybe a little longer depending on your oven. This can be served with or without a glaze topping. Or, with fruit to the side. Or, with a pile of ice cream. Any way you slice it, it's scrumptious! It might also help to ask Deb's mom to join you in spirit. Hers never fell flat!

Dear God ...

About the Author

Mary-Ellen Low

Mary-Ellen Low has been a nurse in the field of long term care nursing for more than thirty years. She lives in West Virginia with her husband, Bob, and her two rescue dogs, Tilly and Bella. House motto: Dogs rule!

About the Illustrator

Nicole Rose

Nicole Rose has been a long-term care nurse for eleven years. She lives in West Virginia with her husband, Ernie, and her five wonderful children. Art has been her passion since childhood. House motto: God opens doors in miraculous ways.

www.ingramcontent.com/pod-product-compliance
Lightning Source LLC
Chambersburg PA
CBHW071505040426
42444CB00008B/1499